PARTICIPANT

JOHN C. MAXWELL

THE 360° LEADER

DEVELOPING YOUR INFLUENCE *from* ANYWHERE *in the* ORGANIZATION

Contents

Letter from John C. Maxwell

Dear Friend,

Developing yourself and those around you is essential to make a great and lasting impact. The leader sees the big picture, but he or she needs other leaders to help make their mental picture a reality.

You and I are going to embark on a journey of personal growth. In this training course you will be challenged to take the many small steps that lead to success each and every day of your life. You'll learn principles that have been tested and proven again and again.

The time you spend with this material will prove to be a worthy investment. Your organization will benefit as you put these ideas into practice.

I have devoted my life to equipping people, and it is my hope that you will take the *The 360° Leader* training to heart by growing and developing others around you.

Your friend,

John C. Maxwell

Introduction

This book is designed to emphasize what you should learn from the DVDs. As you watch the DVDs, take comprehensive notes in your workbook. Read *The 360° Leader* to gain an even deeper understanding of the principles being taught. In doing so, your understanding of this subject will grow.

After you have completed this book, it can serve as a helpful reference guide as you consider your responsibility as a leader/team member and how to improve as you function in that role. Approach this course with the understanding that, upon completion, you have the knowledge to help make yourself into a better leader.

The Myths Often Believed by Those in the Middle

The Law of Influence:
The True Measure of Leadership Is Influence — Nothing More — Nothing Less.

1. The ____________ Myth: "I can't lead if I am not at the top."

Five Levels of Leadership

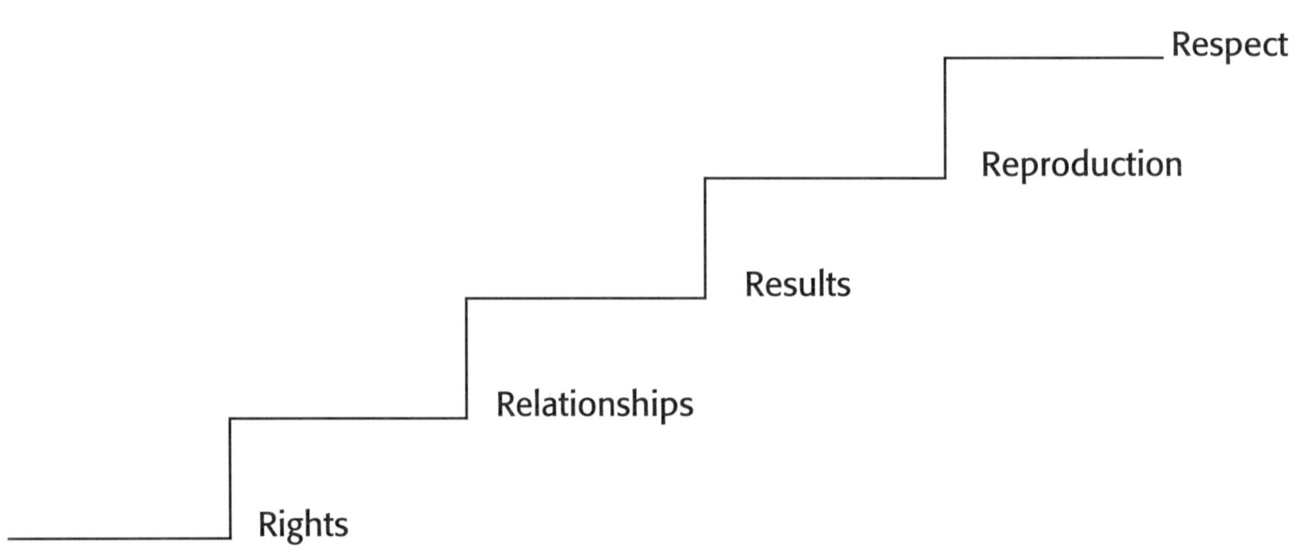

"To do nothing in the middle is to create more weight for the top leader to move. For some leaders — it might even feel like dead weight. Leaders in the middle can have a profound effect on an organization."

— David Branker

Leadership is a ___________ you make, not a ___________ you sit.

2. The _______________ Myth: "When I get to the top, then I'll learn to lead."

The Law of Process:

Leadership Develops Daily, Not in a Day.

"When opportunity comes, it's too late to prepare."

— John Wooden

3. The _______________ Myth: "If I were on top, then people would follow me."

People who have no leadership experience have a tendency to _________________ the importance of a leadership title.

The Law of Buy In:

People Buy Into the Leader, Then the Vision.

A _____________ doesn't make a leader, but a ____________ can make the position.

You may be able to grant someone a position, but you cannot grant them real leadership. Influence must be earned.

4. The ________________ Myth: "When I get to the top, I'll be in control."

The Law of Sacrifice:

A Leader Must Give Up to Go Up.

The Myths Often Believed by Those in the Middle, continued

5. The ____________ Myth: "When I get to the top, I'll no longer be limited."

In many organizations, as you move up the ladder, you may even find that the amount of responsibility you take on increases faster than the amount of authority you receive.

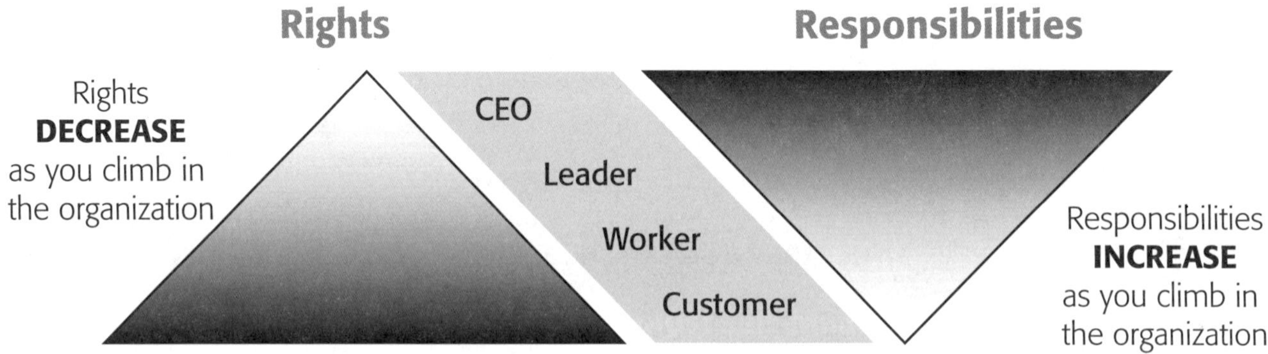

The Law of Empowerment:
Only Secure Leaders Give Power Away.

6. The ____________ Myth: "I can't reach my potential if I'm not the top leader."

Reality: __________ people will never be the _________ leader in an organization.

I believe that people should strive for the top of their game, not the top the organization.

Only when leaders in the middle reach their potential, will the leader at the top reach his or her potential!

The Law of the Inner Circle:
A Leader's Potential is Determined By Those Around Him.

7. The ____________________ Myth: "If I can't get to the top, then I won't try to lead."

I believe that individuals can become better leaders wherever they are. Improve your leadership, and you can impact your organization. You can change people's lives. You can be someone who adds value. You can learn to influence people at every level of the organization — even if you never get to the top. By helping others, you can help yourself.

The Law of E. F. Hutton:
When the Real Leader Speaks, People Listen.

Here is a brief review of the Seven Myths every leader in the middle faces:

Myth #1 **The Position Myth:** "I can't lead if I am not at the top."

Myth #2 **The Destination Myth:** "When I get to the top, then I'll learn to lead."

Myth #3 **The Influence Myth:** "If I were on top, then people would follow me."

Myth #4 **The Inexperience Myth:** "When I get to the top, I'll be in control."

Myth #5 **The Freedom Myth:** "When I get to the top, I'll no longer be limited."

Myth #6 **The Potential Myth:** "I can't reach my potential if I'm not the top leader."

Myth #7 **The All-or-Nothing Myth:** "If I can't get to the top, then I won't try to lead."

The Challenges 360° Leaders Face

1. The ____________ Challenge: The pressure of being caught in the middle

The Key to Successfully Navigating the Tension Challenge:

Learn to lead with the ________________ others have placed on you.

How to Relieve the Tension Challenge

It's not enough to merely recognize that leading from somewhere in the middle of an organization can be stressful. It's not good enough to simply survive. You want to thrive, and to do that, you need to learn how to relieve the tension.

Five Suggestions for Relieving the Tension Challenge:

(1) Become ________________ with the ____________.
Comfort is a function of __________________ and ____________ your position.

"How often I've been put to the test
To make the best of second-best,
Only to wake one day and see
That second-best is best for me."

— Helen Laurie

(2) Know what to _________ and what to _________ _________.

(3) Find __________ ____________ to answers when caught in the middle.

(4) Never violate your ____________ or the __________ of the leader.

If you want to know what will increase the Tension Challenge to the breaking point, it's violating the trust given to you with your authority or position. That can mean abusing the power of your position, intentionally undermining your leader, or using the organization's resources for personal gain. David

Branker, executive director of a large organization in Jacksonville, Florida, said, "Trust is built one block at a time, but when it is violated, the entire wall comes crashing down."

(5) Find a way to relieve ____________.

2. The ________________ Challenge: Following an ineffective leader

The Key to Successfully Navigating the Frustration Challenge:

Your job isn't to fix the leader; it's to __________ ___________. If the leader won't change, then change your attitude or your work address.

The Solution to the Frustration Challenge: Adding Value

A normal reaction to the Frustration Challenge is to fix or replace the leader you're working for, but that is usually not an option for leaders in the middle of the pack. Besides, even if it were, it would be inappropriate. No matter what our circumstances, our greatest limitation isn't the leader above us — it's the spirit within us.

Remember, your leadership is as much disposition as position. The role of leaders in the middle of an organization — in nearly every circumstance — is to add value to the organization and to the leader.

(1) Develop a ___________ _________________ with your leader.

(2) Identify and appreciate your leader's _______________.

(3) ____________ ______________ to adding value to your leader's strengths.

(4) Get _______________ to develop a game plan to complement your leader's ________________.

(5) Expose your leader to good leadership _______________.

(6) _____________ ____________ your leader.

The Challenges 360° Leaders Face, continued

3. The ______________ Challenge: One head … many hats

The Key to Successfully Navigating the Multi-Hat Challenge:

______________ what hat to put on and then ______________ the challenge.

Demands from Leaders at the Top

Demands from Customers

Leaders in the Middle

Expectations from Vendors

Expectations from Followers

Hat Suggestions

(1) Remember that the hat sets the ____________ when interacting with others.

(2) Don't use one hat to accomplish a task required for ____________ ________.

(3) When you change hats, don't change your ______________.

(4) Don't neglect ________ ________ you are responsible to wear.

(5) Remain ____________.

Only ___________ and ___________ people are continually flexible.

4. The ________ Challenge: You're often hidden in the middle

The Key to Successfully Navigating the Ego Challenge:

Remember that ________________ good leadership does get noticed.

> *"True heroism is remarkably sober, very undramatic.*
> *It is not the urge to surpass all others at whatever cost,*
> *but the urge to serve others at whatever the cost."*
>
> — Arthur Ashe

The Challenges 360° Leaders Face, continued

How to Handle the Ego Challenge

(1) Concentrate more on your ___________ than your ____________.

"There is a man in the world who never gets turned down,
wherever he chances to stray;
He gets the glad hand in the populous town,
or out where the farmers make hay;
He is greeted with pleasure on deserts of sand,
and deep in the aisles of the woods;
Wherever he goes there is a welcoming hand —
he's the man who delivers the goods."
— Walt Whitman

(2) Appreciate the __________ of your position.

Not everyone will understand or appreciate the work you do. So it's important that you do. A cute anecdote from Nobel Prize winner Charles H. Townes illustrates this well. Townes commented: "It's like the beaver told the rabbit as they stared up at the immense wall of Hoover Dam, 'No, I didn't actually build it myself. But it was based on an idea of mine.'"

(3) Find satisfaction in knowing the _________ ___________ for the success of a project.

(4) Understand the difference between _________-promotion and _____________ promotion.

Self-Promotion	vs.	Selfless Promotion
______________-First		______________-First
______________ Up		______________ Up
______________ Information		______________ Information
______________ Credit		______________ Credit
______________ the Ball (star)		______________ the Ball
______________ the Ball (blame)		______________ the Ball
______________ Others		______________ Others

Self-promotion says, "If you don't toot your own horn, no one will toot it for you." Selfless promotion says, "I just want to help the team make beautiful music!"

5. The ______________ Challenge: Leaders like the front more than the middle

The Key to Successfully Navigating the Fulfillment Challenge:

Leadership is more ______________ than position — influence others from wherever you are.

Why Leaders Like the Front

There are advantages to being in front or on the top of an organization. But the same things that can benefit leaders can also make leadership difficult. It is almost always a double-edged sword, and anyone who sees only the positives without recognizing the negatives is either naive or inexperienced.

The Challenges 360° Leaders Face, continued

How to Be Fulfilled in the Middle of the Pack: See the Big Picture

Education pioneer Henrietta Mears said: "The person who keeps busy helping the one who is below him won't have time to envy the person above him."

(1) Define a win in terms of ______________.

Legendary basketball coach John Wooden said: "The main ingredient of stardom is the rest of the team."

(2) Engage in continual __________________.

The person in the middle of the team is usually in the middle of the communication.

(3) Gain _______________ and _____________.

In *The Autobiography of Harry Golden,* the author wrote: "The arrogance of the young is a direct result of not having known enough consequences. The turkey that every day greedily approaches the farmer who tosses him grain is not wrong. It is just that no one ever told him about Thanksgiving."

"Maturity doesn't come with _________.
It begins with the acceptance of __________________."

— Ed Cole

6. The ___________ Challenge: Championing the vision is more difficult when you didn't create it

The Key to Successfully Navigating the Vision Challenge:

The more you ___________ in the vision, the more it becomes your __________.

How People Respond to the Vision Challenge

(1) __________ ________ — criticize and sabotage the vision.

Why? They didn't help ____________ it.

(2) ____________ ________ — do their own thing.

(3) ______________ ________ — leave the organization.

(4) ___________ _________ ________ — find a way to align with the vision.

(5) _______________ ________ — take the leader's vision and make it a reality.

Vision begins with one person but it is only accomplished by many other people.

Those Who Championed the Vision	Those Who Did Not
Placed the ____________________ needs first.	Placed their __________ needs first.
Kept the ___________ before the people.	Kept ________________ before the people.
Represented ______ well to others.	Represented ________________ well to others.
_________________ their role.	____________________ their roles.

(6) Add ___________ to it.

The Challenges 360° Leaders Face, continued

7. The ______________ Challenge: Leading others beyond your position is not easy

The Key to Successfully Navigating the Influence Challenge:

Think influence, not position.

As you have heard about the previous six challenges, perhaps you have felt that their impact on you is minimal. If so, you can consider yourself fortunate. Nobody, however, escapes the Influence Challenge, no matter how wonderful an organization you work for or how great your boss is. Leading others beyond your position is not easy. If real leadership were easy, anybody would do it, and everyone could excel at it.

Most good leaders believe in themselves and their leadership. They are confident that if others would follow them, then the team would benefit and accomplish its goals. So why doesn't that always happen? Why don't people who report to them line up to follow? Because they don't have to! Leadership is influence. If you have neither position nor influence, people will not follow you. And the further outside your position they are, the less likely they are to let you lead them. That's why 360° Leaders work to change their thinking from, *I want a position that will make people follow me to, I want to become a person whom people will want to follow.*

(1) People follow leaders they know — Leaders __________ __________.

"You cannot antagonize and influence at the same time."

— John Knox

(2) People follow leaders they trust — Leaders __________ ________________.

Political theorist Thomas Paine said: "I love the man that can smile in trouble, that can gather strength from distress, and grow brave by reflection. 'Tis the business of little minds to shrink, but he whose heart is firm, and whose conscience approves his conduct, will pursue his principles unto death." What gives a leader the strength to exhibit such admirable qualities? The answer is character.

(3) People follow leaders they respect — Leaders who are ______________.

Respect is almost always gained on difficult ground. A leadership position will help a leader only until difficulties arise. Then the leader must arise to meet those difficulties. Leaders who are incapable of meeting challenges may desire respect from their followers and peers, but they rarely get it.

While poor leaders demand respect, competent leaders command respect.

(4) People follow leaders they can approach — Leaders who are ______________.

(5) People follow leaders they admire — Leaders with ______________.

Here is a brief review of the challenges every leader in the middle faces:

1. **The Tension Challenge:** The pressure of being "caught in the middle."

2. **The Frustration Challenge:** Following an ineffective leader.

3. **The Multi-Hat Challenge:** One head…many hats.

4. **The Ego Challenge:** You're often hidden in the middle.

5. **The Fulfillment Challenge:** Leaders like the front more than the middle.

6. **The Vision Challenge:** Championing the vision is more difficult when you didn't create it.

7. **The Influence Challenge:** Leading others beyond your position is not easy.

The Principles 360° Leaders Practice to Lead Up

"Follow me, I'm right behind you."

1. Lead _____________ exceptionally well.

The key to leading yourself is to learn ____________________.

Decision making is _____________.

Decision managing is _______________.

What A Leader Must Self-Manage

(1) Manage your _____________.

Good leaders know when to ___________ emotions and when to __________ them.

Whether you delay or display your emotions should not be for your own gratification. You should ask yourself, *What does the team need?* not, *What will make me feel better?*

(2) Manage your _________.

"Until you value yourself, you won't value your time."

— M. Scott Peck

(3) Manage your _____________.

_________ of the time — Work where you are strongest.

_________ of the time — Work where you are learning.

_________ of the time — Work in other necessary areas.

(4) Manage your ____________.

The ABCs of energy-drain:

Activity without ______________ — Doing things that don't seem to matter.

Burden without ____________ — Not being able to do things that really matter.

Conflict without ________________ — Not being able to deal with what's the matter.

(5) Manage your ______________ _________.

Success is having those closest to me __________ and ____________ me the most.

If you want to lead up, you must always lead yourself first. If you can't, you have no credibility. I've found the following to be true:

If I can't lead myself, others won't follow me.

If I can't lead myself, others won't respect me.

If I can't lead myself, others won't partner with me.

2. Lighten your leader's __________.

How Often You Lift	How the Leader Responds
__________ ________ __________	"Thanks."
__________ __________	"I need you."
________________	"Let me help you."

The Principles 360° Leaders Practice to Lead Up, continued

How to Lift Your Leader's Load

(1) Do your own job __________.

Hall of Fame baseball player Willie Mays said: "It isn't hard to be good from time to time in sports. What's tough is being good every day."

(2) When you find a ____________, provide a ____________.

(3) Tell leaders what they __________ to hear, not what they __________ to hear.

Because of their intuition, good leaders often see more than others see, and they see things before others do.

Why? Because they see everything from a leadership bias. But if the organization they lead gets large, they often lose their edge. They become disconnected. What is the remedy to this problem? They ask the people in their inner circle to see things for them.

(4) __________ ________ for your leader whenever you can.

Helping your leaders means supporting them and standing up for them whenever you can. Former army general and U.S. secretary of state Colin Powell said: "When we are debating an issue, loyalty means giving me your honest opinion, whether you think I'll like it or not. Disagreement, at this stage, stimulates me. But once a decision has been made, the debate ends. From that point on, loyalty means executing the decision as if it were your own."

(5) ________ your leader how you can lift the load.

3 Questions I Ask the Leader Before Speaking

1. "Can I say something that *you have said* before to give you ____________ voice?"

2. "Can I say something that *you would like to say but can't*, to give you a ___________ voice?"

3. "Can I say something that *you haven't said* yet to give you the __________ voice?"

3. Be willing to ________ what others ___________.

Few things gain the appreciation of a top leader more quickly than an employee with a whatever-it-takes attitude.

What It Means To Do What Others Won't

(1) 360° Leaders take the ___________ __________.

The ability to accomplish difficult tasks earns others' respect very quickly. In *Developing the Leader Within You,* I point out that one of the quickest ways to gain leadership is problem solving.

(2) 360° Leaders succeed with _____________ ___________.

(3) 360° Leaders put _______________ on the line.

(4) 360° Leaders do __________ than _____________.

Expectations are high for people at the top. And, unfortunately, in many organizations the expectations for people at the bottom are low. But expectations are mixed in the middle.

4. Do more than manage, __________.

"Leaders must be good managers, but most managers are not necessarily good leaders."

— Tom Mullins

The Principles 360° Leaders Practice to Lead Up, continued

Leadership is more than management. Leadership is:

- ___________ more than projects.
- ______________ more than maintenance.
- _________ more than science.
- _____________ more than formula.
- ___________ more than procedure.
- _________ more than caution.
- ___________ more than reaction.
- _________________ more than rules.
- who you _________ more than what you do.

Moving Beyond Management

(1) Leaders think ________________.

(2) Leaders see within the ____________ _____________.

Most people evaluate events in their lives according to how they will be personally affected. Leaders think within a broader context. They start by asking themselves, *How will this impact my people?*

(3) Leaders __________ ________________.

Some people ask questions — ________________.

Some people ask questions and have answers — ____________ ________________.

Some people ask questions, have answers and take responsibility — _______________.

Some people ask questions, have answers, take responsibility and influence others to follow — __________ _____________.

(4) Leaders invest power in _____________.

Management is often about control. Managers have to control costs, control quality, control efficiency. That's one reason why some good managers have a difficult time making the paradigm shift to leadership. Leading isn't about controlling; it's about releasing.

5. Invest in relational ________________.

The only way to influence those above you is by connecting with them. Relationship skills define 360° Leaders and separate them from other leaders. Remember, people won't go along with you if they can't get along with you.

(1) Listen to your leader's ________________.

Heartbeat Signals:

(1) _____________

(2) _______________

(3) _____________

(4) _____________

The Principles 360° Leaders Practice to Lead Up, continued

(2) Support your leader's ___________.

Each time another person in the organization embraces the vision and passes it on, it's like giving the vision "fresh legs."

Promote your leader's dream and your leader will promote you.

(3) Earn your leader's ___________.

"Loyalty publicly results in leverage privately."

— Andy Stanley

(4) Learn to work with your leader's ________________.

Sales expert and author Les Giblin said: "You can't make the other fellow feel important in your presence if you secretly feel that he is a nobody." Likewise, you can't build a positive relationship with your boss if you secretly disrespect him because of his weaknesses. Since everybody has blind spots and weak areas, why not learn to work with them?

The thesis of *Winning With People* is that people can usually trace their successes and failures to the relationships in their lives. The same is true when it comes to leadership. The quality of the relationship you have with your leader will impact your success or failure. It is certainly worth investing in.

6. Be prepared ___________ __________ you take your leader's time.

(1) ___________ 10 X.

You show your value when you show that you value your leader's time. The best way to do that is to spend ten minutes preparing for every minute that you expect to meet. Management author Charles C. Gibbons confirmed this when he advised, "One of the best ways to save time is to think and plan ahead; five minutes of thinking can often save an hour of work."

(2) Don't make your boss __________ for you.

How Leaders at the Top Think When They Receive Questions From Leaders in the Middle:

- If they ask questions because they can't think, then we're in trouble.
- If they ask questions because they're lazy, then they are in trouble.
- If they ask questions so that everyone can move faster, then we're headed for success.

(3) Bring something to the __________.

"A gift opens the way for the giver and ushers him into the presence of the great."

— Proverb

(4) Give a ___________ on your leader's investment.

Courtney McBath: Every time we meet he says…

- Here's what you said the last time we met.
- Here's what I learned.
- Here's what I did.
- Did I do it right?
- Can I ask you more questions?

The Principles 360° Leaders Practice to Lead Up, continued

7. Know when to __________ and when to __________ __________.

When To Push Forward

(1) Do I know something my boss doesn't, but ___________ _________ ___________?

(2) Is time _____________ _________?

Constantine Nicandros, president of Conoco, said: "The competitive marketplace is strewn with good ideas whose time came and went because inadequate attention was given to moving rapidly and hitting an open window of opportunity. The same marketplace is strewn with broken glass of windows of opportunities hit after they were slammed shut."

(3) Are my responsibilities at __________?

When your leader entrusts you with tasks, you have a responsibility to follow through and get them done. If you are having difficulty with that, most leaders I know would rather know about it and have an opportunity to help you accomplish them than see you work all by yourself but fail.

When to Back Off

(1) Am I promoting my own ____________?

From the perspective of leaders at the top, organizations have two kinds of leaders in the middle: those who ask, "What can you do for me?" and those who ask, "What can I do for you?" The first are trying to ride their leaders — and any colleagues or employees they find useful — to the top. The second are trying to carry their organization — along with its leaders and others they can help — to the top.

(2) Have I already made my __________?

"You do not lead by hitting people over the head — that's assault, not leadership."

— Dwight Eisenhower

(3) Does my request exceed my ________________?

8. Become a __________ player.

The Law of the __________:

Winning Teams Have Players Who Make Things Happen.

(1) Go-to players produce when the _____________ _______ ________.

There are many different kinds of people in the workplace, and you can measure them according to what they do for the organization:

What They Do	Kind of Player
Never deliver	____________________
Sometimes deliver	____________________
Always deliver when in their comfort zone	____________________
Always deliver regardless of the situation	____________________

(2) Go-to players produce when the ______________ _________ _________.

(3) Go-to players produce when the ______________ _______ _________.

The Principles 360° Leaders Practice to Lead Up, continued

3 Kinds of People When It Comes to Momentum

(1) Momentum ______________

(2) Momentum ____________

(3) Momentum ____________

I love a sign I saw at a small business called "The 57 Rules to Deliver the Goods." Beneath the title it read:

Rule 1: Deliver the Goods

Rule 2: The Other 56 Don't Matter

That's the philosophy of go-to players. They deliver no matter how tough the situation is.

9. Be better ______________ than you are __________.

The key to personal development is to be more ____________-oriented than __________-oriented.

(1) The better you are, the greater your __________ today.

I love this quote from Elbert Hubbard: "If what you did yesterday still looks big to you, you haven't done much today." If you look back at past accomplishments, and they don't look small to you now, then you haven't grown very much since you completed them. If you look back at a job you did years ago, and you don't think you could do it better now, then you're not improving in that area of your life.

(2) The better you are, the greater your ______________ for tomorrow.

Mahatma Gandhi: "The difference between what we do and what we are capable of doing would suffice to solve most of the world's problems."

(3) The better you are, the greater the potential of ___________ for tomorrow.

Jack Welch said: "Before you are a leader, success is all about growing yourself. When you become a leader, success is all about growing others." And the time to start is today.

Review:

Before you begin to learn what it takes to lead across, review the nine principles you need to master in order to lead up:

1. Lead yourself exceptionally well.
2. Lighten your leader's load.
3. Be willing to do what others won't.
4. Do more than manage — lead!
5. Invest in relational chemistry.
6. Be prepared every time you take your leader's time.
7. Know when to push and when to back off.
8. Become a go-to player.
9. Be better tomorrow than you are today.

The Principles 360° Leaders Practice to Lead Across

"Follow me, I'll walk with you."

What distinguishes a merely competent leader from one who goes to the next level? Competent leaders can lead followers. They can find, gather, recruit, and enlist them. This is no easy task, but a leader who can lead only followers is limited. To make it to the next level of leadership, a leader must be able to lead other leaders — not just those below them, but also those above and alongside them.

1. Understand, practice and complete the ________________ __________.

Many people who have difficulty leading across have trouble because their approach is too shortsighted. They try to gain influence too quickly. Leading is not a one-time event; it's an ongoing process that takes time — especially with peers.

If you want to gain influence and credibility with people working alongside you, then don't try to take shortcuts or cheat the process. Instead, learn to understand, practice, and complete the leadership loop with them.

The Leadership Loop

Take a look at the following graphic, which will give you an idea of what the leadership loop looks like:

1. ______________

2. ______________

3. ______________

4. ______________

5. ______________

6. ______________

7. ______________

(1) Caring — Take an ____________ in people.

People always move toward someone who increases them and away from anyone who decreases them.

(2) Learning — Get to __________ people.

(3) Appreciating — ____________ people.

(4) Contributing — _________ __________ to people.

Few things increase the credibility of leaders more than adding value to the people around them.

(5) Verbalizing — ___________ people.

Affirm means to __________ _________.

(6) Leading — _____________ people.

(7) Succeeding — ____________ with people.

Great leaders don't use people so that they can win. They lead people so that they all can win together.

2. Put _______________ fellow leaders ahead of ______________ with them.

There's nothing wrong with competition. The problem for many leaders is that they end up competing against their peers in their own organization in a way that hurts the team and them. It all depends on how you handle competition and how you channel it. In healthy working environments, there is both competition and teamwork. The issue is to know when each is appropriate. When it comes to your teammates, you want to compete in such a way that instead of *competing* with them, you are *completing* them. Those are two totally different mindsets.

The Principles 360° Leaders Practice to Lead Across, continued

Competing vs. Completing

Competing	Completing
____________ Mindset	______________ Mindset
________-First	__________-First
____________ Trust	____________ Trust
Think Win-__________	Think Win-_________
___________-Thinking (My Good Ideas)	____________-Thinking (Our Great Ideas)
_____________ Others	_____________ Others

Winning at all costs will cost you when it comes to your peers. If your goal is to beat your peers, then you will never be able to lead across with them.

3. Be a ___________.

Author Richard Huxley said:

> "A true friend is one who hears and understands when you share your deepest feelings. He supports you when you are struggling; he corrects you, gently and with love, when you err; and he forgives you when you fail. A true friend prods you to personal growth, stretches you to your full potential. And most amazing of all, he celebrates your successes as if they were his own."

4. Avoid office _____________.

"Playing politics" is changing who you appear to be or what you normally do to gain an advantage with whoever currently has power.

Two Ways to Get Ahead

There seem to be two main paths for people to get ahead in organizations. One way is to try to get ahead by doing the work. The other is to try to get ahead by working an angle. It's the difference between production and politics.

People Who Rely On Production	People Who Rely On Politics
Depend on how they ___________.	Depend on who they ___________.
Focus on what they _________.	Focus on what they _________.
Become better than they ____________.	Appear better than they __________.
Provide _______________.	Take _______________.
Do what's _______________.	Do what's _____________.
Work to control __________ own destiny.	Let ____________ control their destiny.
___________ into the next level.	Hope to be ___________ the next level.
Base decisions on _______________.	Base decisions on ______________.

The Principles 360° Leaders Practice to Lead Across, continued

The bottom line is that people who might be described as "political" are ruled by their desire to get ahead instead of a desire for excellence, productivity, teamwork, or consistency. Whatever values and skills they have are secondary to their ambition. And while they sometimes appear to get ahead, their gains are always temporary. In the long run, integrity, consistency, and productivity always pay off — in better teamwork and a clear conscience.

To Avoid Politics…

(1) Avoid ____________.

It's been said that great people talk about ideas, average people talk about themselves, and small people talk about others.

(2) Stay away from ___________ ________________.

(3) Stand up for what's __________, not just for what's _____________.

(4) Look at _________ sides of the argument.

Before you have an argument with your boss, take a good look at both sides — his side and the outside.

(5) Don't _____________ your turf.

Politics is often about power. Political leaders protect whatever is theirs because they don't want to lose power. If they lose power, then they might not win. And as I already mentioned, winning is their primary motivation. People who want to win at all costs fight and scrap to keep everything that belongs to them. They fight for their budget. They fight for office space. They guard their ideas. They hoard their supplies. If it belongs to them, they protect it.

5. ___________ your circle of acquaintances.

How to Expand Your Circle

(1) Expand beyond your __________ __________.

To get outside of your comfort zone, why not start with those in your comfort zone? Every friend you have has a friend you don't have.

(2) Expand beyond your _____________.

(3) Expand beyond your ______________.

6. Let the _________ idea win.

What Leads to the Best Ideas?

To let the best idea win, you must first generate good ideas. And then you must work to make them even better. How do 360° Leaders do that? How do they help the team find the best ideas? I believe 360° Leaders follow this pattern:

(1) 360° Leaders listen to __________ __________.

(2) 360° Leaders ____________ creative people and their ideas.

Ideas are such fragile things, especially when they first come to light. Advertising executive Charlie Brower said: "A new idea is delicate. It can be killed by a sneer or a yawn; it can be stabbed to death by a quip and worried to death by a frown on the right man's brow."

(3) 360° Leaders don't take rejection ______________.

The Principles 360° Leaders Practice to Lead Across, continued

Following is a list of the last nine trade books I've written. Of those, I've selected the title of only one.

The 360° Leader	I wanted to call it *Leading from the Middle of the Pack.*
25 Ways to Win with People	Les Parrott came up with the concept and title.
Winning with People	Charlie Wetzel came up with that title.
Today Matters	I wanted to call it *The Secret of Your Success.*
Thinking for a Change	I wanted to call it *Thinking Your Way to the Top.*
The 17 Essential Qualities of a Team Player	The team at Thomas Nelson picked that title.
The 17 Indisputable Laws of Teamwork	I got to pick the title of this book!
The 21 Indispensable Qualities of a Leader	The concept and title were developed in a joint marketing meeting.
The 21 Irrefutable Laws of Leadership	The concept and title came from Victor Oliver, my editor.

7. Don't pretend you're ____________.

"Nothing would get done at all if a man waited until he could do something so well that no one could find fault with it."

— John Henry Cardinal Newman

How to Be "Real" in a Competitive Environment

(1) Admit your ___________.

(2) Ask for ___________.

(3) Worry less about what ___________ ___________.

One of the nice things about being imperfect is the joy that it brings to others!

The _____________ Principle: Each person we meet has potential to teach us something.

Review:

Before you begin learning about leading down the 360° Leader way, review the seven principles you need to master in order to lead across:

1. Understand, practice, and complete the leadership loop.
2. Put *completing* fellow leaders ahead of *competing* with them.
3. Be a friend.
4. Avoid office politics.
5. Expand your circle of acquaintances.
6. Let the best idea win.
7. Don't pretend you're perfect.

The Principles 360° Leaders Practice to Lead Down

"Follow me, I'll add value to you."

Leadership is traditionally thought of as a top-down activity. The leader leads; the followers follow. Simple. If you have been leading others for any length of time, you may be tempted to skip this section of the book, thinking, *I already know how to do that.* I don't want you to miss something really important, however. Because 360° Leaders are by definition nonpositional — they lead through influence, not position, power, or leverage. And they take that approach not only with those above and alongside them, but also with those who work under them. This is what makes 360° Leaders unique — and so effective. They take the time and effort to earn influence with their followers just as they do with those over whom they have no authority.

1. __________ ____________ through the halls.

How?

To connect with people, you travel at their speed. When connecting with your leader, chances are you need to speed up. Though it is not always true, in general the higher you go in an organization's hierarchy, the faster the leaders travel. The leader at the top often has boundless energy and is very quick mentally.

Conversely, when you move down, people move more slowly.

(1) Express that you __________.

First, and foremost, leadership is a people business!

(2) Pay attention when people start _____________ you.

(3) Tend to the ____________ and they will _________ to the business.

What 360° Leaders All Have in Common:

Despite their passion for the vision and their love of action, they give the majority of their effort to the people. Leaders who tend only to business often end up losing the people *and* the business. But leaders who tend to the people usually build up the people — and the business.

2. See everyone as a "________."

Questions

- Who gets my best effort? The leader who believes I'm a 10 or the leader who believes I'm a 2?
- Who do I enjoy working with? The leader who believes I'm a 10 or the leader who believes I'm a 2?
- Who is the easiest for me to approach? The leader who believes I'm a 10 or the leader who believes I'm a 2?
- Who wants the best for me? The leader who believes I'm a 10 or the leader who believes I'm a 2?
- Who will I learn the most from? The leader who believes I'm a 10 or the leader who believes I'm a 2?

360° Leaders get more out of their people because they think more of their people.

If you want to really shine in this area, apply the following suggestions when working with your people:

(1) See them as who they can ____________.

(2) Let them _____________ your belief in them.

The Principles 360° Leaders Practice to Lead Down, continued

(3) Catch them doing something __________.

(4) Believe the best — Give others the benefit of the __________.

(5) Realize that "10" has many ______________.

3. ___________ each team-member as a person.

How To Develop Your People

Before I make a few recommendations about how to develop others, I need to make clear the difference between equipping people and developing them. When you equip people, you teach them how to do a job. If you show someone how to use a machine or some other device, that's equipping. If you teach someone how to make a sale, that's equipping. If you train them in departmental procedures, that's equipping.

You should already be providing training to your people so that they know how to do their jobs. Equipping should be a given (although I know that not all leaders do this well).

Development is different. When you develop people, you are helping them to improve as individuals. You are helping them acquire personal qualities that will benefit them in many areas of life, not just their job. When you help someone cultivate discipline or a positive attitude, that's development. When you teach someone to manage their time more effectively or improve their people skills, that's development. When you teach leadership, that's development. What I've found is that many leaders don't have a developmental mindset. They expect their employees to take care of their developmental needs on their own. What they fail to realize, however, is that development always pays higher dividends than equipping because it helps the whole person and lifts him to a higher level.

Development is harder to do than equipping, but it is well worth the price. Here's what you need to do as you get started:

(1) See development as a ______________ ____________.

(2) Discover each person's ____________ and ____________.

"Ignore what a man desires and you ignore the very source of his power."

— Walter Lippmann

(3) Lead everyone _______________.

If you desire to be a 360° Leader, you need to take responsibility for conforming your leadership style to what your people need, not expecting them to adapt to you.

(4) Use organizational goals for ______________ ________________.

- When it's bad for the individual but bad for the organization, _____________ ___________.
- When it's bad for the organization but good for the individual, the __________________ __________.
- When it's bad for the individual but good for the organization, the ________________ __________.
- When it's good for the individual and good for the organization, ______________ _________.

The Principles 360° Leaders Practice to Lead Down, continued

4. Place people in their ____________ zones.

"Only _________ of workers, work in the areas of their strength."

— *Now, Discover Your Strengths,*
Marcus Buckingham and Donald O. Clifton

The number one reason people don't like their jobs is that they are not working in the area of their strengths.

Successful ___________ find their own strength zones.

Successful ____________ find the strength zones of the people they lead.

Two of the most important questions to ask are:

What am I doing to develop myself?

What am I doing to develop my staff?

The first question determines your personal potential and ongoing capacity to lead. The second determines the potential of your team.

The Law of the Niche:
All Players Have a Place Where They Add the Most Value.

5. __________ the behavior that you desire.

What I Am	What I Do	Results
Character driven	Do right	__________
Relational	Care	__________
Encourager	Believe in people	__________
Visionary	Set goals	__________
Student	Learn	__________
Inspiring	Motivate	__________
Selfless	Focus on others	__________
Confident	Make decisions	__________

Leaders need to be what they want to see.

The Law of ______________:

We Attract Who We Are, Not Who We Want.

6. Transfer the __________.

Though leaders in the middle may not always be the inventors of the vision, they are almost always its interpreters.

The Principles 360° Leaders Practice to Lead Down, continued

A Check-List for Transferring the Vision

(1) ____________

When preparing to cast vision, ask: What do I want them to know and what do I want them to do?

(2) ________________ of past, present, and future

When people are able to touch the past, they will be more inclined to reach for the future. Anytime you can show that the past, present, and future are unified, you bring power and continuity to your vision casting.

(3) ____________

Although vision tells people where they need to go, purpose tells them why they should go.

(4) ___________

(5) A _______________

(6) ____________

Stories __________ — Principles _________

(7) ____________

If there is no passion in the picture, then your vision isn't transferable.

7. ___________ for ___________.

Principles to Follow When Rewarding for Results

(1) Give praise _____________ and _____________.

"It's okay to let those you lead outshine you, for if they shine brightly enough, they reflect positively on you."

— Billy Hornsby

(2) Don't reward everyone the __________.

"Any business or industry that pays equal rewards to its goof-offs and its eager beavers sooner or later will find itself with more goof-offs than eager beavers."

— Mick Delaney

(3) Give perks ____________ pay.

Review:

Are you relying on influence to lead down as a 360° Leader should? Review the seven principles you need to master in order to lead down:

1. Walk slowly through the halls.
2. See everyone as a "10."
3. Develop each team-member as a person.
4. Place people in their strength zones.
5. Model the behavior you desire.
6. Transfer the vision.
7. Reward for results.

Notes

Notes

Need More Workbooks?
Do You Need a Facilitator Guide?

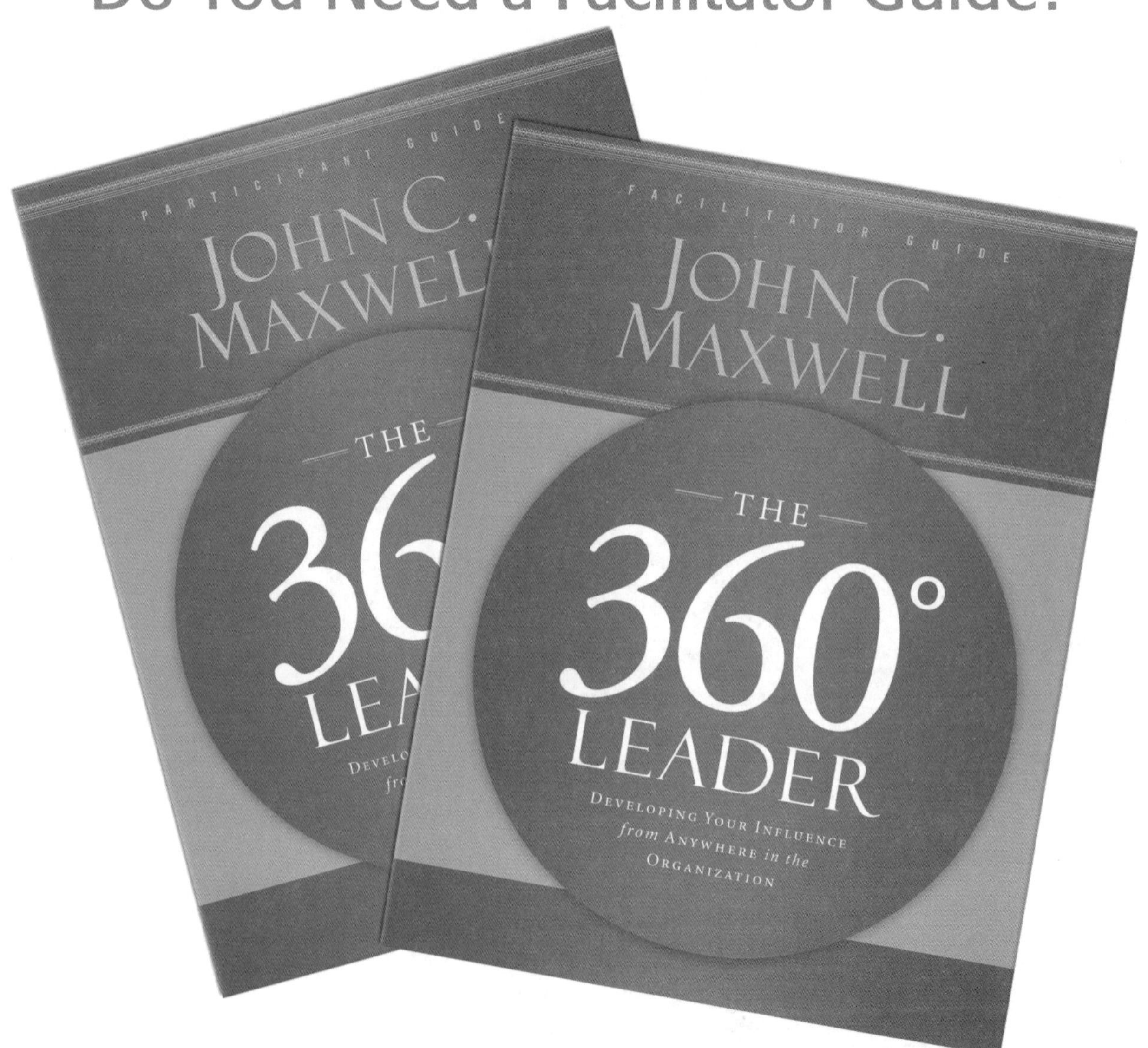

Order these resources online at MaximumImpact.com